Earth on Earth

In Bin Ramke's striking new poems, a richly sparse, taut lyric carves wondrous paths between poetic, scientific, and spiritual methods of knowing, of presenting and being present in a vanishing world. Ever inquisitive, gracefully encyclopedic in his range of reference, Ramke, with Stevens sewn into his coat pocket, breaks open etymology, faith, childhood, personhood, gardens that may be our last. In *Earth on Earth*, imagination reigns as companion and guide, no matter the botch we've made of our planet. Here, we may have "beaten our swords into cellphones" but all is alive, vibrant with "momentary sense, tense/ in its eager return-wish// to return to earth a sense/ of spring, a metallic torsion." *Earth on Earth* is wrenching and brave in its quest to know our unfathomable future.

GILLIAN CONOLEY

author of *A Little More Red Sun on the Human:*
New and Selected Poems

What can be said of earth on earth? Bin Ramke's *Earth on Earth* isn't interested in answers, but sonic embodiments, linguistic mirroring, and metaphysical music that invites us to behold: "a way to say / is a way to see." The work in this collection rides a whirlwind of fact and occult conjecture into delightfully allusive airs. As readers, we find ourselves in a new neural capaciousness, "the brain beyond itself," beside itself, ecstatic, remembering a bayou, a dead brother, an asteroid, a word slipping out time. Poem by poem, Ramke perpetuates a haunted present into a future that is achingly imminent, god-shaped and "god-sharpened."

CHRISTINE HUME

author of *Saturation Project*

The title of Bin Ramke's collection *Earth on Earth* signals an intent to take what tends earthward as so many mirror-inverted ascents of sense. 'We want to fall,' the poet writes, but instead 'we walk radiant,' aligned away from the center of a world lost in space. Here is a Lucretian meditation on the melody and melancholy of matter; here is a memory-haunted review of the 'body parts' of language; here is a word-music played in a minor key, a night-cry replete with intricate trickeries of sound and syntax. Bin Ramke joins the ranks of Rilke and Stevens as a writer of philosophical lyric.

ANDREW JORON

author of *The Absolute Letter*

Earth on Earth

Earth on Earth

POEMS

BIN RAMKE

OMNIDAWN
OAKLAND, CALIFORNIA   2021

Cover art by Mia Mulvey

Text set in TT Marxiana

Cover and interior design by adam b. bohannon

Library of Congress Cataloging-in-Publication Data

Names: Ramke, Bin, 1947- author.
Title: Earth on earth : poems / Bin Ramke.
Description: Oakland, California : Omnidawn Publishing, 2021. | Summary:
"A kind of translation of a thousand-year-old poem, "Earth took of Earth,"
this book is an attempt to restate in personal, emotional terms a sense
of both danger and of consolation from earth itself. Many of these poems
arose during a collaboration with the ecologist-ceramicist Mia Mulvey:
her work with earth, clay often extruded through digitally guided
machinery, continually rhymes with Ramke's attempts to understand
damages done, but also to celebrate the facts of earth-as, for instance,
that geosmin, the scent of wet soil, is so recognizable even in trace
amounts. The title of this book is a play on the phrase "heaven on
earth": no, the very best-and it is a lot-to hope for is earth on
earth"– Provided by publisher.
Identifiers: LCCN 2021032375 | ISBN 9781632430991 (paperback)
Subjects: LCGFT: Poetry.
Classification: LCC PS3568.A446 E27 2021 | DDC 811/.54–dc23
LC record available at https://lccn.loc.gov/2021032375

Published by Omnidawn Publishing, Oakland, California
www.omnidawn.com   (510) 237-5472
10 9 8 7 6 5 4 3 2 1
ISBN: 978-1-63243-099-1

for Linda and Nic

For Linda and Will

I too rest on a thought,
indeed on a single word
that already
at one of its ends
is beginning
to cease to be

"This Hour"

MARIN SORESCU (TRANS. MICHAEL HAMBURGER)

CONTENTS

I

Midmourning   17

Toy Time   18

Camera Obscura (The Outside In)   20

Danses Sacrée et Profane (Debussy 1904)   22

The Past   24

Material Science   25

Black Painting, Black Dog   28

The Garden the Family   29

Varieties of Light   31

After "Owl's Clover" by Wallace Stevens   32

Spirit Level   33

Literate of Air   34

II

Fall   39

There Is No Consolation without Delight   40

A Flight of Days   42

They Are Like Grass   43

Yesterday When It Is Past   44

Secret Sins in the Light   45

Fear of Floating   46

"Tune a Brook by Moving the Stones in It"   48

"The Snow Is a Form of Light"   50

Nights of Sleep, Nights of Not Sleep   52

Phrase Book   53

Argument and Value, x and y   55

After Turner ("Sunrise with Sea Monsters")   56

Sentence Passed and Passing   57

Applied Astronomy   58

Insert Illustration Here   61

III

Flesh of the Word Game   65

Eye and Mind Game   66

"In Certain American Games in Which There Are To Be Partners"   67

Asbestos   68

In a Game Played by the Chaga   71

Body Parts   72

Avian Warning/Morning   73

Jesus Speaks to the Daughters of Jerusalem   74

Partial   76

A Change in Climate   78

Thingness. A Many-Body Problem   80

Lucretian Origami   83

IV

Beetles from Horses (after Wang Wei)   89

The Waiting and the Wisdom Wanting   92

Earth A: Three Meditations on Matter   93

Earth B: Where to Live   96

Garden Symmetries   100

I

Suppose we try to recall a forgotten name. The state of our conscious-
ness is peculiar. There is a gap therein ; but no mere gap. It is a gap
that is intensely active....If wrong names are proposed to us, this singu-
larly definite gap acts immediately so as to negate them....And the gap of
one word does not feel like the gap of another, all empty of content as
both might seem necessarily to be when described as gaps.

The Principles of Psychology

WILLIAM JAMES

Midmourning

My brain here next to me
like a cat on the keyboard
makes only accidental music
of absence—abstract,
meditative, morose.

The memory is no mirror,
myself as the perceived self,
no other; or: the perceiver
is the god of self, solemn
deity saying small things

as if large, at large, loud
things in a small voice. Not
mirrored, not dependent upon

angles of incidence. Only
begetter of angled reflection,
the brain beyond itself.

Toy Time

Proportional to the play space time

proceeds; the child tricks itself
into adult, adulation—being grown
up is a place, a geometrical reversal.
For instance watch the circling
revelation of a dog descending
into sleep, "dog" being a metaphor
for love. Child. Wait, we watch

in the night for gods to descend
bedazzled like a ten year old's
blue jean jacket. Example:
I had as a companion in the doll
house a small fox terrier, toy
of toys, a pet with a name alive
during the toy hours

as outside the play room weather
continued impervious to mind of
child the weather was as weather
will be imperious of will. The fox
terrier tick tocks her way across

the tin floor of the tiny house filled
with what is, what will be.

I work this way now, small bits
like minutes, like, inches onward.

Camera Obscura
(The Outside In)

after Abelardo Morell

Nothing   *Your remembrances are like unto ashes,*
comes of   *your bodies to bodies of clay.*
nothing   *Job 13:12*
but also everything

I can claim a dirty world as home, as only home
available, filled with a parity of trees and shrubs
completed by the birds of the air, the worms
winged, and the wildering acts of my fellows.

Making shapes of mud, the masters
the children and the animals turn the world
they find into homes and hollows,
at least for the night: I watched my dog
dig then lie contentedly down.
Consider movement, dirt upward
into tree onward into apple. Once started
it has never stopped, this cycle,
of carbon and air and anxiety: trembling

on a precipice of being, a system
builds itself, a leaf the legitimate heir

to the nothingness out of which
the light arises airy each morning.

Close your box of bricks against the light
then open one small hole, and the world enters
upside down, to entertain, to be held among us.

Danses Sacrée et Profane
(Debussy 1904)

The violinist's sinister fingers
a pale half-
spider wrapping a fly

the gods sharpen knives
at that angle of bow to strings
bowing a sound like laughter
where the mouth parts weave
text textures textiles
golden orbs

confess is to commit
as confection is to confine,
saith the preacher.

Ours as an age of truth
is why we lie
so readily, so well
the chosen animal
who lies beside us
and speaks when spoken to,

leaves webbish tracings
amid the dust after
and of.

Mute is to mutilate
as love is to levitate
saith the spider.

The Past

is what we thought
it was. As in a sin.

Now that you are the oldest
in the room, what
future beckons?

We know that cloud and clod connect electric
trickily the charge shadows itself
plus and minus

until a spectacular
spark leaps I did once drop
into a ditch to save my head.

No breeze to speak of today,
ripples raised in the birdbath by
the drinking of a wasp a witness

the present tense of wasp
comfort in spite
of heat and the danger.

Material Science

Leggi nel verde alloro she sang

WOODWORK

The tree lives, the table
remembers. A limb
suffices, cut and pasted.

The mind embraces
as if an arm surrounds
while brain branches

into memory.
Biology is not so hard
as wood, would it not

be for a need
we have for names:
elm, birch, past, perfect.

BARK

Aspen as a single
life surging upward millennially
upon which lovers wrote brutal
language love as two curves cut

plus a plus sign and initials
induce anguish legible if not
forgivable. The incision

of self into other self
brings blood, binds, blinds, maddens,
as cited operatically:

Orlando destroyed them all,
arborglyphs which would have killed
over time, consumed by one man's
mind carving a name in skin
of living trees, dying stones
the landscape

RAIN, RANDOM ACTS
(Central Park 1978)

A color of men and boys awash in wind
a walk along a lake, a pond:
clouds aground, reflections also of trees
to confound us all.

It is the time when parks turn dangerous
we are told—signs warn against staying here
where fellow humans hide shadowed.
There is plenty to fear in fall.

Still a heron finds fish. Still
long-legged birds turn a time or two
toward where frogs might be
while night noises start:

"start" as in startle? Star, art.
Fish jump. Insects. A sudden sound.

for Mia Mulvey

Black Painting, Black Dog

Fifty years after his death his paintings were taken
from his house, the painted walls of the Villa
of the Deaf Man, Goya having lived in silence (or what
I who do not live there call silence) since age forty-six
(Susac's syndrome or Cogan's syndrome
likely explanations) but the dog, the dog who

looks up who is nearly lost in the umber and gray,
between sheets of brown only his head apparent,
unknown unnamed and merely a smear of black
with a nose no noise no bark (some assume he slides
under sand or dirt I do not) no known response

to his unknown condition. Paint dries silent as sand
upon the plane like whispers of refusal like
sleeping dogs which do not lie but tell
only truculent twitching and snorts.

The Garden the Family

1

Heterotopias are places with special rules that provide them with a certain degree of autonomy. None of what happens there would be understandable in another context. Examples of such places include cemeteries, psychiatric hospitals, the theatre, the cinema, the garden...the family

YORJANDER CAPETILLO HERNÁNDEZ

2

We still have a long way to go to cross the garden given our weight of wealth plus memories against us like wind as if we were butterfly already not unspeakable caterpillar still.

3

Another way to see it is to think of wasps buzzing in tune around the lips of bottles tossed. Floral filters abound. Home or not the next turn in the garden path we take and don't forget the snacks.

4

I do know better than this so what, live a life ready or not. Remember *red light* when someone's sister stood then turned and caught you moving you were sent back to begin again you who wanted nothing but to impress her just a little there on the lawn the long shadows before you.

5

To be a child is one thing to have one another who fills the neighbors with dread yet some sounds at play in the morning are pleasant they

make us feel at home. A morning of play, Saturday, and the radios loud
on the window sill

6

while everywhere glitters sprinkled irrigation.
A sun makes a sound against.

7

Someone's sister explained to you how disappointing it is to finally
reach those clouds the edges blurred the feeling not of lightness of
light but of a dreary morning soon to rain she had ridden in an
airplane you had not yet. No one had yet died in your life.

8

Hollyhocks tower petunias quiver marigolds welter beneath the trees
while some small rodents cringe.

9

Personally, I like a garden to provide shade and a soft place to
nap, even though quiet is a form of terror. Listen to the blab of the
pavement even as you maneuver the footpaths, steppingstones and
Japanese bridges—every bone a bell ringing itself silent.

10

One evening I watered plants and noticed three bats circling the
house—more accurately, doing figure eights involving our house and a
neighbor's tree. I saw all clearly outlined against a lingering sky then
remembered Rilke, that zing and crack of porcelain....   Meanwhile in
the house the light was yellow and leaking onto the lawn. The wet lawn.

Varieties of Light

Look. Winged creatures convene
beyond, buoyant in air, on
waves of substance beyond
visible. The olm, Proteus
Anguinus, lives without light
but lives in waves, light
in weight delicatest wavelet
of water. His minuscule legs
and chordate construction
provide pale flight for the fleet
of watery foot, cave confined.

What ancestor would return
into day with that message?

After "Owl's Clover"
by Wallace Stevens

Gardening is a way of coming to something other than terms with
the world underfoot. I am looking at this moment at a morning glory
which circumnutated itself onto the lawn and is twining up a seed
stalk of grass. I see one heart-shaped leaf some five inches across.
I see several similar leaves shredding and tattered, and I see the
beetle responsible, glittering in sunlight. The insects this area—a
small property, a house and a yard dense with plants to pour scarce
water upon, water recently melted from snow in the mountains—are
phenomenally numerous this summer: flies of a dozen different species,
wasps and white-faced hornets and bees foreign and domestic—
especially small green ones, and big ones with hairy feet—and moths
and butterflies and gnats and four-spotted skippers and terrifying
things which lay eggs in the living bodies of terrifying things.

Here is what I can hear at this moment: a fixed-wing aircraft, a
helicopter, a lawnmower, cars on the interstate, a few nearby flies
flying, a squirrel stripping limbs of a berry-laden tree, a chickadee
splitting sunflower seeds, scattering lesser seeds beneath her for the
rats which have taken to burrowing under the riches of this corner of
the city. I cannot hear the rats.

Owl's clover is a plant, hemiparasitic. It's inflorescences are said to
resemble the beak of the owl.

Spirit Level

"Seeing Mountains, Seeing Water," 2002, Li Shurui

Consider that we, like water, align with earth's
center of gravity: we walk radiant from the point
four thousand miles beneath us. We want to fall;
we step instead.

                    Stopping to look across a lake
a woman becomes an eye, momentary.
She sees a mountain float fractured across
a surface, flat planes connect then dissipate.

Then she makes a thing, a thin thing
of nearly nothing.

Her geometry flutters in wind, mosquito-
netting formed into cubes by bamboo,
wet, immersed in the lake to make the shape

of the nearby shoreline. Unlivable houses
except they are themselves a kind of life,
spirited, enspirited by the watery airs

arising around us, watchers. We fail
to see because we fall, friendly enough
but our language is wrong.

Literate of Air

To write

The baby's rattle teaches through the hand
the vibration and the vision

a mystery; with the maker of the sound,
pebble or bone or BB, hardly
heard nor seen becomes

to swerve, to serve...

What we see is never
seen by others, was
the sum of the forces
felt by ear or eye indifferently

I read too much and slept
when the chance arose, or fell

as the twilight filled with shuddering
movement of small bits of air
bright

Brownian motion writing itself
into last rays of sun a linger
of meaning

a lingering of moaning or mourning
as a way to reenter the world

of the sighted, sighed my uncle,
the blind one who made music
for a living, who lived among us
nephews and nieces who

received small records as gifts

disks he made with the latest
machines he used a brush to clear
the wax blond string curling off the surface

this before the digital
sound the waste

matter of talk, the terror of sight
muffled by affliction. His friend
spoke sign to the hand, his hand

upturned to receive the massage,
the comfort, or the hope
we had to spare I wish

I could tell
to him "Eye Music" a poem,   *Ella Mae Lentz*

the ecstasy of the telephone wire
rising falling seen from the car

on the road trip the child
the body the pulse of the mother's
arms, but of the view all

all is vibration, of the eye, the ear,
the palm of the hand, the engine

the photons
the touch is all as
tender tantrum.

II

Earth laid earth in an earthen trough

Fall

a slow drip of leaf
a twig like a leaky faucet
one drop per year

tree is a trick as a
trick of light
a tree falls every

century rots
roots and all
speedy spadesful

in the forest a sound
astounding silence
failed leaf left

like turbulence a crowd
behind
less loud than

There Is No Consolation
Without Delight

1

The gods I know are not asleep
their eyes are closed

the farther the view
the sharper the vision

each thing has a voice
called resonant frequency

as a child I wanted a headache,
a thing my mother had often

I did in late evening hear and see
the mullet leap and splash

bayou is a word from Choctaw
which gives me pleasure

Borges drew his self-portrait
after his blindness

"yellow...has remained faithful"
Borges lost the vision of colors

consecutively, gradually—
the shorter wavelengths

later. And yet *shade* means absence
of light (or presence of color).

2

Figurative use in reference to comparative obscurity is from 1640s.
Meaning "a ghost" is from 1610s; dramatic (or mock-dramatic)
expression *"shades of _____ "* to invoke or acknowledge a memory is from
1818, from the "ghost" sense. Meaning "lamp cover" is from 1780. Sense
of "window blind" first recorded 1845. Meaning "cover to protect the
eyes" is from 1801. Meaning "grade of color" first recorded 1680s; that
of "degree or gradation of darkness in a color" is from 1680s (compare
nuance, from French *nue* "cloud"). Meaning "small amount or degree"
is from 1782.
http://www.etymonline.com/index.php?allowed_in_frame=0&search=shade

A Flight of Days

after Psalm 90

A number picked as in a trick, amusing,
somewhere between one and a hundred, discrete
or transcendent. To fly is a trick of the night
called dream, but we really did that time

when you in my dream not young
were without age—not mind or meaning.
I had been reading somewhere the temperature
of the earth, the temperature of ice
when it becomes sentient and feels pain

I had been reading there how the days
of our years are threescore years and ten;
and if by reason of strength they be
fourscore years, yet is their strength
labour and sorrow;
for it is soon cut off, and we fly away.

What is reading but dreaming of flight
and I watched from the ground
my years in fear of woven light and air.

They Are Like Grass

The work of our hands when we have
no hands; we spend our days as a tale
that is told, completed before. So
while we wait we make things, small
things that click or sing to us. Crickets
of straw and string. Plucked.

Another thing to do is think
but the glitter of horizon
casts bright shadows against us
thus we must watch closer
think more finely like children

even though the number of our days
diminishes, like light like little toys
made of leftover light.

Yesterday When It Is Past

Would you if you could live
to be a thousand? Think of the candles.
Think of which windows will have broken.

I was remembering today
a path along a bayou I walked watching
snakes swim across, two snakes across water

gray, the snakes and the water, a gray
mud of watery light against the stars from
the stars that evening as I made a way home

thinking in spite of the snakes and the water
of only light like candles consuming
themselves wickedly wrong.

Secret Sins in the Light

To live in the garden for snails
and slugs under moonlight could be
a form of reading, script shining

but I do not welcome the homely
art of eating and touching light lighter
than any braille-reading finger the face

of the soil. *Soil* was as word once
the place where the wild boar wallowed.
His homely comfort.

Fear of Floating

the autography—the self-writing—of the water
on the boundary between the finite and the infinite

BERNHARDT SIEGERT

I wanted to build a boat.
A large enough shadow is a kind of day
within which work is cooler
than during those desiccant
      days under sun

when the wooden shape slips
across clay into the stream itself slipping
across the clay shape
      at the bottom of

water. The world casts a shadow
which I saw last week the moon red
and round looking ball-like up there
frightening a little
      since it seemed

fallable. Floating seen from beneath
a round boat of red riders above us ignorant
but wistful, wistly
      waiting for the fall.

Is shadow matter? It does but
consider the self a generator
of shadow—all aside, a self
forms a flatness
          on the wall.

As epistemic things, then, ships were submarines....
All ships emerge from under water

          *

And I wanted to feel the form
arise between my hands, as the pottery
spinning contains an emptiness
unlonely filled with future.

A boat like a museum a place
to live, contained. In a bottle
sails and spars rise at the pull
of a string, Marionette made

to dance a kind of life like
shadows on the wall the accident
of nightlife in the city the streets
full of emptiness which expands

the writing hand on the wall the hull
the Plimsoll line the barnacles beneath
waving their terrors, wafting.

"Tune a Brook
by Moving the Stones in It"

Scratch Music, S,

CORNELIUS CARDEW

The sounds of American rivers
roughly write in sand and mud.

One never pictures oneself purely
in the sound of one's voice

Another listens, leans
in order to see his face floating

Bird call shimmers
against the reflected ears in bird baths

Thoreau spoke of the extra eye
the spot of reflection on the water surface

A voice called across water (for
instance, your mother your name)

Wide water percussive stirred
into concert

Even a small river can make large
sounds as long as time as wide

The words music and musical
can be used like clay or clarity

A whistle or hiss or whisper
can be a concert, a certainty contested

Like water passing past
a flood louder than allowed

"The Snow Is a Form of Light"

—YVES BONNEFOY

The more grotesque bats—say,
for instance, ghost-faced—
form a streaming live sporadic
river of airborne cave born
mammal visible against
the Rilkean evening sky. Careened
out of the grotto.

Herd life is like light. Literary paperish
sounds descend from bat onto boy watching
who thinks his ear feels air batted downward;

he does, he hears the insect eaten, its little light
doused like flame beneath the altar boy's douter,
a wisp left of sound, unsound. Beauty in the bat
is a smokelike smear against light twice

daily, arriving and departing regular as weather,
cloudish particulate buzzing out of caves carved
airish.
                          But snow is white and cloud-
formed and falls not angular but parabolic

meaningful storied fallings soft then deathful
like power functions swerving into then out

of the picture. To fall to then ablate or melt
or change phase form water to chaos to gas
a skier knows the earth by touch and
tangent, the surface rises and rounds
to fall with white weather

                              a woman
in Seattle designs gardens and watercourses
did for a dead princess make an oval
of water winding on sounding surfaces
to flourish under sun and cold because
she knows the body bends
to the gravity of soil and the grave's body

becomes airs and waters but the surface
of air the bottom edge of air in which we
swim is a boundary a little like a lake.
Of light. Like snow the particles fly
but all do fall.

                                        for Kathryn Gustafson

Nights of Sleep, Nights of Not Sleep

That evening I watered plants and noticed
three bats about the property—their figure-
eights involved my house and a neighbor's.
Against the thin screed of light
outlined I saw their sharp darkness
void of detail—invulnerable flyers, magnificent
abated, fluttering cracks in the continuum.

I have been witness to the world in the way
any stone in the stream has been to water.
Imagine the bat imagining. Bats and whales
my cousins, potential poets feasting
on tiny life, mumbling among
themselves, flattering none.

Phrase Book

Play hardens into knowledge

HUIZINGA

Leaf readers (tea, tree,
book (1 leaf 2 pages))
leave sound to wither

diaphragm-powered language
versus verses written
such different lairs of sense

linger in memory (hums
of bees as a kind of mind)
readers report on a future

find solace there where once
we went with confident out-
passing of ports after storm

an asteroid is among us
is us mother to us mingled
masses of earth gathered

like signatures sewn
an asteroid came calling
the trees did burn the fish

did drown the air did burn
and small life smoldered

like birds
who exhaled the last
of atmosphere another world
among us a world a way.

Argument and Value, X and Y

Sinusoidal functions describe anything
wave shaped with respect to place or time.
$y = a \sin(bx+c)$, where a, b and c are constants.
x in, y out. Say for instance I am walking
along the Gulf of Mexico, somewhere near
the Texas and Louisiana state line,
and the clouds on the horizon gather
crowding each other into shapes
amplitude angular velocity and phase angles
shift shapes and yet the night still comes.

Say I am still walking but a decade in time
has passed and ships and families of fish.
The sky is darker, the night still comes.
Say X is a century, or a thousand years
it doesn't matter. A woman stands
on the beach, it is late, the sun low
and her shadow sharply points east
but the ratio of the height of the woman
to her line of sight to the tip of her shadow

is related to the rate of the waves washing
her feet. Every curve a caress.

After Turner
("Sunrise with Sea Monsters")

Who loves without knowing how
you are loved without knowing
we have not met the sun follows you
down streets in winter its cold gold
a terror to some a joy to some

the moon follows me around the sun
all the year it whirls spiraling
unaware unconcerned a puppy
keeping its one face turned properly
is what it is like to love

this is what it is to be unloved but
unconcerned: to wander following
the days and leaves turning forgetting
age forgetting that once without
pain there was no reason

to fear the shapes clouds could assume;
I could live there another life if offered
in the cave of that cloud, there.

Sentence Passed and Passing

"...the words for 'innocent,' apart from their legal use, develop, through
'harmless, guileless,' a disparaging sense 'credulous, naïve, simple, foolish.'"

CARL DARLING BUCK

To be sentient is to pass sentence, she said in my dream

as the timorous morning washed through
a window like a light flood. I've lived in cities
prone to flooding, proclivitied toward watery fates:

own little and learn to swim. But mud remains
while mold makes way in the woodwork and under
papered walls. An innocent aware only of a small past
full of water and woodwork, I share
defeat, defined by water, by bayous
and bays through which things drained,

drowned things, battered things, lost things borrowed
nor returned by rights. Things of the theorized
landscape, things of the hushed and haunted, specular.

That's the kind of bystander I was, believing
even the water held blameless in the lung
in the languishing rooms, the refuges lost.

We stood on the bridge and watched it become
an island in this the city of thirst.

Applied Astronomy

A

I once understood that which now bewilders;
to bewilder is the desire, astronomy
the goal. To know a star for an origin

I said: Just as well go with astrology,
accept an ancient name a direction through the void,
assume a link between birth and belief.

My sense of time and place contingent, a falling
into contact—being lost. To lose one's way is
revelation, in reverse. I chose to study animals next:

I remember a certain shady green road (where I saw a snake)
and a waterfall, with a degree of pleasure, which must be
connected with the pleasure from scenery, though not directly
recognized as such. The sandy plain before the house has left

a strong impression, which is obscurely connected with an indistinct
remembrance of curious insects, probably a Cimex mottled with red, and
Zygaena, *the burnet-moth.*

Autobiographical Fragment, 1838)

CHARLES DARWIN

I did once wish to know to finally
know the names of trees I climbed,
to call the names of the birds I bothered,

to pronounce the Latin lists while peering through
lenses. All this and more was possible
if contingent. Next came chemistry,
a place of white coats and dark odors

of transmutations deep as adolescence
when the touch of one's own skin turned utterly
false, utterly necessary. I would pour deeply
any old self into shiny new bottles, if I could
fit, final yet alive there. There in my closet
resistant to naphthalene, tiny moths abound.

$C_{10}H_8$, all it takes is a little carbon, less hydrogen,
a couple of benzene rings. You can find it in walnuts.
Juglans regia, for instance, with seed in its shell
like brain in its skull and might as well
be used to treat my illness, my fanciful
self. To chew these little organs knowing.

B
We have beaten our swords into cellphones
and I in charge of my own mind, minding
and mending the universe as I see it, as I see fit.

Let us imagine an astronomer earlier than Copernicus, reflecting upon
the system of Ptolemy; he will notice that one of the two circles, epicycle
or deferent, of each of the planets is traversed in the same time. This
cannot be by chance, there is therefore among all the planets
I know not what mysterious bond.
The stars chase each other inscribing curves of pursuit across our

skies, our visions of the ancient arrival of light of light in the night. I want to hold Lampyridae in one hand, Sirius, Canopus, and Rigel in the other. Everything the same size held at arm's length. Sun and moon, heaven and earth, named and unnamed.

Copernicus, by simply changing the coordinate axes that are regarded as fixed, makes this appearance vanish; each planet describes only one circle and the times of revolution become independent . . .
(H. Stein, *Physics and Philosophy Meet*)

c

Ratios linger. Some stars evaporate,
others coalesce into small stones
to rattle under streams in the mountains.

Insert Illustration Here

My little unit-circle life
a life-like life subtending
terror and tendencies
sines and cosines, sins
and sentences. Imagine
here a drawing, a circle
and a triangle and
an arrow pointing.

Birds inhabit.
To the west
their feathers are red,
to the east yellow.
This is a description.

III

Here, the philosopher, by tightly binding time, memory, and imagination, affirmed that only beings that perceive time can remember, and they do so with the same faculty with which they perceive time, that is, with imagination. Indeed, memory is impossible without an image . . .

Nymphs

GIORGIO AGAMBEN

Flesh of the Word Game

I argued with my brother and my brother died.
I said Line cannot be seen it is a concept.
He said Can you concede there is a line
under that thing of graphite on the page?
I said No not so simple.

His death came thirty years later unconnected
to our arguing. He died of cigarettes and knowing
better. His engineering helped the moon landers
land. He read poetry in secret but without belief.

I love what I love and live for more. Politics
is impolite. There are approaches to life and
there are exits. "Alas" derives from Latin for "weary."

Eye and Mind Game

I saw my sisters dance and knew the game.
It was a dance of hands, intricate and fatal.
It is a forfeit game like the German *Alle*
Vögel fliegen, for instance. Two stand
facing each other each claps her hands
.then each clap two hands against the others'
then each claps her own hand against hand
then both clap right against other's right
hand then each claps her own hand against
her other hand then both clap left hand
against other left hand then again each
claps together her own hands
then again both clap two hands
against other's two hands in this way
they proceed cyclically unto
failure the one to err first forfeits her life.

"In Certain American Games in which there Are to Be Partners

lengths of string are passed through the crack
of a closed door; on one side are boys,
on the other girls. When each girl and each boy
have grasped the end of a string,
the door is opened and the players
holding the same string are partners."

"Itkonen describes the Lappish thread game:
children have pieces of thread, three for each six
players, one of whom takes the threads, folds them, holds them so that
both ends protrude. The others take hold of the ends. Those who have
caught hold of the same thread start running."

Studies in Cheremis, Vol 6, Games

Asbestos

Supposed in the Middle Ages to be salamanders' wool; another old name for
it in English was fossil linen *(18c.). Prester John, the Emperor of India,*
and Pope Alexander III were said to have had robes or tunics made of it.

ETYMONLINE.COM

Formal fashion a clothing
consolatory and defensive

a mineral defense against
personal inflammation against

the flambeaux parade's
soft hissing fingers pickpockets

in the crowd, the crowd
cries for coin the children

the foreignness of this love,
this beloved of the night

inflammatory, an amorous mixture
of exotic and lewd; a rock

can be woven fibrous into
potholders and flame-proof suits

that act of touch
the sense of touch or taste or tenderness

momentary sense, tense
in its eager return-wish

to return to earth a sense
a spring, a metallic torsion

of desire versus not-desire
contentment contained:

pleasure is a staleness like virtue
not virtue as strength but virtue

versus, the minerals in our water
made us famous brought

the world here to bathe
and to drink our minerals of an evening

when tendrils tend
to rise from the surface, breathable,

picturesque, then gone, vaporish
like fire a song sold.

As children poured lighter
fluid in our palm, set it aflame,

we might not hurt
then again we might.

In a Game Played by the Chaga

players hand in hand pass through the door
made by the clasped and uplifted hands
of two leaders who capture the last in line.
When all have been caught but one the one
redeems the rest by asking the doorkeepers
to give him a child to carry water for him,
another to hoe his garden, another to gather
wood, another to watch over his slaves
to punish any who hope to escape.

Body Parts

There are three body parts: top,
bottom, and middle.
There are seven types of fusion: cold,
warm, hot, north, south, young, and old.

These are the ages of anxiety: the sixties,
twelve as a new birthday approaches,
and old, all numbers greater than mine.

The numbers of the angels are engraved
thusly: first, and first, and first, and....
However freely we translate, the French
for seventy is rendered only one way.
The number of the stripes of the lily
is seventy. The number of a small,
livable country is twelve. Or so.

To number is not to name. The past
is unnamable, and is one. The parts
of the body are beyond reckoning.
The first of the parts of the body is head.
The second is foot. Between is chaos,
which is another word for innumerable.

Avian Warning/Morning

A bird brilliant of mind and beak
brain winged and trilling.
I am awake a wake

of sound on a lake composed
waves of particulate motion
and pain, plainly.

Jesus Speaks to
the Daughters of Jerusalem

It is always about suffering, the pleonastic. We add
words, and in the end all are necessary, none sufficient.

Consider evaporation, the change into gas
by a liquid, the achievement of spirituality.

Marisa Merz wrote a poem: *and in the mind*
pond and sky are a single instant
the two clouds evaporate each other. She turned
"evaporate" transitive. Grammar asserts,

as in whether he spoke to or with the daughters,
who were, assumed, mothers. And later said:

a time will come when the barren alone
will be blessed. Bless, bliss, blood. Whatever is is still
small enough to lose. You know how
the planet Saturn would float pillowish

on our earthly waters. We want a better world
but there is none, there is only the one
which is what we feel. Dogs and cats live here
with us, and they can be happy. As a child

I walked the perimeter of the church, stopped
fourteen times to contemplate suffering
serial suffering including three falls and
tortures and one death and a body removed

with tenderness. But there were offers of help,
and the suggestion that all would be well.

Partial

A leaning toward, a segment-
ation. Some troubling partial
differential equation becomes

a portion of, say, a life: to be
partial to. However
well lived at its end

as if it never was
as if a life could exist without
the one who lived it as if

I did not know how to live
as two, so I would pretend
one was not me at a time,

the other a visitor. Treat visitors
well, incline toward their wishes,
offer breakfast in bed.

*

At any age an end is available
*I didn't really need to know that,
but it does no harm*

MALTE LAURIDS BRIGGE

to fill full the wanton
particulate evening a
soft light and hard

landing speak to self
about self then write
backward in the mirror.

Others do otherwise,
wisdom being a piece
of the jigsawed image.

We have machines to do that
for us, to find the places
worth severing, severally.

If to be impartial is
to be whole, to be partial
is to be biased, then

to suffer does not suffice,
will not serve, however severely
wished, whistled for.

A Change in Climate

Cold is our element and winter's air
Brings voices as of lions coming down
"The Sun this March"
WALLACE STEVENS

I escaped The South in search of Winter,
a lauded elemental out of books, the blended
terms of Time like leaves from trees failing, falling—

I knew The Tropics and other secrets. I would watch
stains on a ceiling green with Time, gardenish
and the mildew harvests itself humbly.

A dangerous time when poets believe themselves.
More visible than We had hoped to be;
We dress this way, and wander among
ourselves picking hairs off our sweaters.

Discard the outer garments as air
encases us more firmly, more fittingly.
There is snow rising in the mountains, falling.
There is something to hope for, far.

We could not invent this world no matter
how thick our arrogance grew in its
manure. We think hard while ink stains

our hands more visibly than blood on
Pilate's. Or Lady Macbeth's? There is water enough

geosmin fills the head with hope, simple bacteria $\rightarrow$
$C_{12}H_{22}O$ ... we learn early to mimic
a healthy world, to smell like (im)mortality.

Thingness. A Many-Body Problem

How many electrons does it take to make a thing?
If one is enough, there is a God; if not, not.

We have discovered the size of the god: Wigner crystals
are small, black holes big, for instance.

I am evaporating on the page in front of you, before
your eyes, before the sentence completes itself.

How many things does it take to make an angel?
One, one supposes, since an angel is not composite

but pure all the way through. When I was a child
computers were people not machines to count

how many could dance. There was a book called
De Thiende, the tenth, about tenthness, a thing.

My mind is not right, but I am not wrong.
Small enough to lose, large enough to miss.

We children said prayers in groups of ten,
a tradition. Decimalization.

A truly small size of angel would make
for a large number dancing, many bodies

on the head of a pin. I have seen it written
by Aquinas that an Angel is a cause, yet (*Summa*, 1,52,3)

Sed Angeli non replent locum, quia solum corpus
replet locum, ut non sit vacuum, ut patet per philosophum,

in IV Physic. Ergo plures Angeli possunt esse in uno loco.
Angels have no size, like life. I have heard it said

that addiction has its own will to live separate
from the addicted. But addiction has no size.

I am writing on the anniversary of the death
of Paul Klee, who drew an Angel with breakfast.

The days on planet Mercury are longer
than the years. I am sitting outside watching

between the movement of surfaces,
air and water, wave, and the light

(wave, particle) in the bowl of the bird bath
a dark design wavers.

A wasp leans itself vertical,
a layer of algae awaits evaporation, prepares.

Oh and also of the planet it was said
"It is not so much an atmosphere as

a slow evaporation of the planet" by
Valeria Mangano, of its exosphere of H and O and

a little He and less Na and K. If I offer
this as a poem and you take it, it is

a gift; if you refuse it is nothing;
its isness is up to you. Vaporous.

"Sin" is a word like "is," cousins
causing self to consider nonself.

Coda: this was my dream: a plant-form
with insects at the tips of the twigs

the limbs stretch forward toward
light, particles stream in the dark.

Space IS more than the place
where things might be;

But the angels do not fill a place, because
only a body fills a place, so that it be not empty,

as appears from the Philosopher (Phys. iv, text 52,58).
Therefore several angels can be in the one place.

Lucretian Origami

One way of thinking is that things fold
and paper is infinitely thin and to be next
to a thing is a kind of being the thing

and another way of thinking is that sound
is alive and then dies like us

*The humming of the bees is heard as the
"voice" of the goddess, and the "sound" of creation*

THOMAS NAIL

*

"I am thinking" is the same as "I spy"
a game of vision, a way to say
is a way to see; the game of children

is a hard one for the child but even more
for adults—who say "sky"

when looking, as the car speeds homeward
hours yet to travel, time to fill.

Another way of thinking is knowing things break
and paper which can tear yet remains puzzled
like a jig-saw completion, ideal. A poem.

The lifetime product of a dozen bees
is a teaspoon of honey. Few humans can match it.

*

My engineer (brother) died
some time ago and yet certain shapes
of air continue of him. As if.

I have his compass, German made, used
for homework—blue velvet interior of
the case worn, the impression of
knurled nobs now permanent in the brown fabric;
mechanical drawing implements leave
a hole in/of air in cases once

con-

taining

stain-

l

ess steel

pencils and protractors.

Protrusible parts leave their marks.

Things and their voices things as their

voices the voice being a vibration even of

fingers leaves a mark in the world even

leaving the world. I helped make clay

apples ceramic shapes molded from   apples

the clay fired the apple eaten

the shape not simple

no two apples

alike.

       *

Folded paper felt by fingers figuring

valley folds mountain folds. But then

origami solves cubic equations

just as straight edge can solve quadratics.

A shape of bird in paper fools no one.

The void of bird a memory of air

paper can be made to fly shaped arrowish

against the air. The air contains constrain(t)s.

Wishes itself, a kind of intelligence
is air swishing against trees and nests.

*

What I told was not a story but a kindness
of words, a word for collections of words,
which is what might   for some be seen as
story, or poem, or   theorem. A word for
words becomes a   companion like dog or
a word for dog—faithful.   The danger in
this kind of thinking—as   when you are in
the train waiting to   begin a journey—is
metaphoric, the danger   is mystical or is
literal or is allegorical.   I leaned into wind
which arose while I was   thinking, then
continued walking   away from the sun
while watching my   shadow lengthen or
appear to lengthen   emblematically or
I watched the slight   darkness I caused
by being a body and   watched the shape
of that darkness   the shape of body. It
moved before me   like a faint god of
the self, the faint self of   traveler. What
is the name for a shape of   self darkened?
It *is* only as comparison.   *Is* in a sense *not*
but is coolness as well as   darkness, felt.

IV

Dirt art. Dirty art. Bogs. Geometric quagmires. Square swamps.

ROBERT MORRIS

postcard February 13, 1967

Beetles from Horses
(after Wang Wei)

Indeed, many creatures naturally
undergo mutation and, when they decay,
are transformed into different species —

for instance bees, out of the rotted flesh of calves,
or beetles from horses, locusts from mules, scorpions from crabs.
wrote Isidore of Seville in his *Etymologies*.

I'll be a park, and thou shalt be my deer
was a way of saying it once when saying
made a kind of being; to be is to altered be

he might have said or sung. When we are sad
we sometimes sing, sound seeming kind
comfort. Comes the deer to my singing.

In my prime I prized alternate taxonomies,
little lists and long murmurations of types
like birds and beetles, plants and platitudes.

I did inform myself with seeing and sometimes
listening, and other times touching. A braille
enthusiasm guided fingers forward filling

the nervous pathways with pity and
patience. A caress contained me, and I
it. Here is another way I was at home:

I walked and felt the little creatures scurry
and sometimes curl into balls beneath my feet,
my careless feet unfeeling. These woods

would resound to the cries of green moss trodden.
The light enters the small forest climbing
the mountain unpeopled

only me who walks while watching light
shine again on green moss. A radio distant
and beyond that an X of contrails

erasing. Clouds have kept me company
while contemptuous deer waved
their tales. Their tails. Their trails

through this small forest marked by dung
and scraps of fur on fir bark. A dog
distantly speaks, or cries—we are warned

not to be curious if a dog barks
in the next village, we are told to
contentedly stay at home. I will

and will become what is necessary: bee,
or butterfly, or beetle rolling his dung ball
by the light of stars out from the green glinted forest.

The Waiting and
the Wisdom Wanting

the bush burned with fire, and the bush was not consumed

Exodus 3:2

A man spoke and a woman spoke and there was no echo
except a sound came from the forest but the forest burned.
A sound is a poem when rightly heard but there was such small
sound then the forest burned.

The burning continued but the bush
was not consumed, or so they said who were not there.

There is said to be wisdom. This is the meaning of scripture,
description. And encryption. But sounds from the crypt continue

and an earth buries us because we buried it.
The logic flawlessly consumes
itself in the fires of forests. All alive breath it;
all who can see see the lovely sunsets.

The birds of the air are messengers, but so is the air.

Earth A:
Three Meditations on Matter

"non-metallic inorganic compounds"

1 THE HALFNESS OF THE MOON

We knew they saw because silence
meant humans drifted to the dark side, voiceless:
Borman, Lovell, and Anders.
Loss of signal at 68 hours, 58 minutes, 45 seconds
into flight when Apollo 8 passed behind the moon.
The first earth animals to look down
upon the moon;
that night we looked up
at the lighted sphere
which seemed a disk, a coin of rock.
Upon the lighted moon we saw
"alliterations of shadows and
of things shadowed," Wallace Stevens (my own
earth upon which I stood).

If there is water on the moon it is not
in the form of water I wash
my face in. Down
at the lighted moon in the bucket
I watch my face and the moon
waver dangerously.

Any child of the south knows
the value of shadow, how the sun
can kill it glitters across
the surface of a small lake
like nothing the moon offered
or ever will. A river is different.

(A little boat can go anywhere
and take me there, he said
his last words, the last to leave).

2 INSTABILITY

even nonmetals may be metals. For example, in certain situations,
you may find metallic oxygen or metallic carbon

ANNE MARIE HELMENSTINE

Calcium is an alkaline earth metal. Hydrogen
in its metallic state is an alkali. Description
as destiny is one way to know a world.

Lithium, sodium, potassium. Pronunciation
as a form of music. The world vibrates when struck.
A string of vanadium stretched across the acropolis

could make a sound in wind. Does, in fact.
To know is to gnaw, said the beetle.

3 THE CERAMICIST WAITS

Hear the molecules mold as material forms:
as she melts earth, her fuel glistens
a cloud of earth a clod confirms
the form she gives—earth took of earth

Erthe toc of erthe erthe wyth woh;   The Ludlow Scribe B,
Erthe other erthe to the erthe droh;   *The Complete Harley*
Erthe leyde erthe in erthene throh;   *2253 MS, vol 2*
Tho hevede erthe of erthe erthe ynoh.

to make a thing, not man, of soil
is to garden or to be a god
or if soil burns and melts
and becomes immortal

that is to be an artist who waits
while matter melts and melds, cools
into comfort, the only we know.

We, made of clay, stand
upon and drink from clay
and shatter.

Earth B: Where to Live

Nathan Isgur, best known for his work on the excited states of the proton and for his role in the discovery of a new symmetry of nature which describes the behavior of heavy quarks

THOMAS JEFFERSON NATIONAL ACCELERATOR FACILITY

Locally Euclidean the land
can be formed and farmed
and still remind us of mind-
made things—the shape as
shape not as thing shaped.
Home is a habit.

A string strummed
is a voice given (allowed at least).

          Imagine
a wave of clay (an earth)
at what speed waves travel
the speed of sound through
home, dirt. Remember a string
a tin-can-telephone tenderly rippling.

(I decided not/decided to write
not a poem about a war not
a war/ it was my time it was about
time and a friend/ when I
was a boy Nathan was good and
kind and scientific; he left this land

he left us for Canada.)
A string is like a line but finite.
Other elementals include
how to make a clay whistle
in the shape of an animal
or perhaps a cloud

                    *

The sound of a bat deafens
while I watch the shape the bat makes,
a crazed astronomy
                    it zigzags through the air
            like a crack through a cup. The way
the track of a bat breaks through evening's porcelain

                                        R. M. RILKE, 8TH ELEGY

against the lighter dark of sky she swerved
stochastic it would seem to the silent
but the flatness of a prairie was

at issue, and how to measure the mind
of a boy who escaped to a northern
realm.
            In your clod of hollow clay make
a beak a mouth then three holes
to make eight notes; to make a hole remove clay
to make a note

start with no holes /*do.*
Cut the first hole / *re.*
Cover the first hole cut a second hole to make *mi.*
Blow into your whistle / *do re mi fa*
cut hole a third hole to enable *so;*
get to *la* by covering the second hole
blowing into your whistle. *Ti*
by covering the first hole leaving two uncovered
as you blow into your whistle.
Leave all holes uncovered and blow
again your whistle for *do* an octave above.

How human it is to name the notes:
as with any physics, what is *isness*; *being*
does not announce itself the same
at all times and turnings—science
tricks itself into being itself.

The names came
from a song to John the Baptist by Guido
of Arezzo, our names for notes.
The song asked god to give us voice
to sing praises. Any thing that is in time
is a voice, a vibration heard by the wise.
Or by the lucky.

Clean the guilt from our stained lips,
O Saint John, it began.

*

The loose string
of/at the end of the universe
to which you attached
your crochet hook...

[MS. Harl. 2253—]
Erþe toc of erþe erþe wyþ woh,
Erþe oþer erþe to þe erþe droh,
Erþe leyde erþe in erþene þroh,
Þo heuede erþe of erþe erþe ynoh.

Earth took earth from earth with woe
Earth other earth to the earth drove
Earth laid earth in an earthen trough
Then earth had of earth, earth enough

(KEY TO THE RIDDLING
line 1: farming, childbirth, etc.
line 2: sex, life in general, etc.
line 3: death, funeral, sex, etc.
line 4: eternity, satiation, salvation, etc.)

Garden Symmetries

(HORTUS CONCLUSUS)

Dike is to ditch as wall is to well.
Hike is to hitch as fall is to feel.

A fox faces a moon, a stuffed
fox faces a neon moon.

Enclosure is luxury; excess, concurrence;
closure is limit, moderation, restraint.

Gethsemane, a garden
invaded by Romans. Prayer and despair.

Rose is to rise as lily is to lie.
Long is to linger as fling is to flick.

Foxes found homes in the cities
like little red orphans.

Fence is to faience as fence is to fence.
A language lingers past the speaker.

Gardens abandoned, love languorous;
children from fairy tales, foreign.

Fear like a native arose
a rose among civilians.

for Gabriel Rico

(OBLIVION)

A form of forgetting? Recall
the farm family against the weather,
the weather long gone, the weather
the great enemy gone replaced
by new weather.

The farm family a figment.
Like the sound the tongue recalls
but not the brain

recalls like the dog hunting furtive
small things in the field
the field a memory of farm
land and life.

My father my mother my brother
My sister of the Bible
my home my minor
desires diminishing.

Personal
and peculiar concepts
arrive in the night.
Soon. Never. Always.

(ACTS OF OBLIVION)

History
the sky is white, she said
when asked

(SOLATIA, EX GRATIA, CONDOLENCE)

Every growing thing, some green

others other. There are eyes better
than ours, one might say, to see. A kind
of shrimp, for one, can see, they say,

colors beyond the human range of sight.
So can crows, who play, like us except
flying. I watched three crows chase

a hawk across the city sky, a daring dance
above my head my walking watching
dance below. Three black points

whirring around the white-gray dash
of hawk. Rough-legged hawk, an arctic
species wintering in Colorado.

Chased out of my vision, vast
nothing of knowledge, erased
geometrical chase point to point.

(THE FORMS OF THE SPIRIT, THE SPARE DENOMINATOR)

And under the firmament *were* their wings straight, the one toward
the other: every one had two, which covered on this side, and every one
had two, which covered on that side, their bodies.   Ezekial 1:23

I speak in one language I think in another.
I hear in a third. My intentions are good.
My hands are tired.

The ancient agreements are call and response.
The new agreements are trifle and tribulation.

I will live this way she said to her mother
while closing the door behind her
her face facing the so-called future, the street.
The places called "private" on the human body
are the places with public functions, where joining
is cause of the future. They are frightening

as winged creatures which crow-like gather,
able to see colors beyond the human range,
able without our mercies, beyond us.

WAITING FOR DAYLIGHT, WAITING FOR THE NIGHT

A great many species of songbirds, perhaps all species, anticipate the
solar day

WALLACE CRAIG

Asleep on the Mississippi all sound is
and even smell is dream, is florid flowering
of small self into the/out of the wound/womb.

the male sings a twilight song both morning and evening,
and in certain important details the order of events
in the morning song is reversed in the evening song

A memory mingled with the future
some manglings, then was lost: what is
called "past"—a pacing as in a waiting room

the latter is a 'mirror image' of the former.
This symmetrical daily cycle anticipates the solar day,
being about 17 minutes ahead...

a palace of pain, a partition of mind
into mourning, morning-after calamity,
the quiet hospitality the smell of ether after

the wood peewee anticipates the dawn by beginning to sing

when the light intensity is ... (about 0.01 foot-candle).

In the evening he anticipates nightfall by ending his song

while there is still considerable daylight (about two foot-candles)"

—"The Twilight Ceremonies of Horseflies and Birds"

Science, 99, February 11, 1944, 125—126

"Explanation" is what we call it, but it is "description" that distinguishes us from older stages of knowledge and science... But how could we possibly explain anything? We operate only with things that do not exist: lines, planes, bodies, atoms, divisible time spans, divisible spaces. How should explanations be at all possible when we first turn everything into an image, our image!

The Gay Science

FRIEDRICH NIETZSCHE (TRANS. WALTER KAUFMANN)

ACKNOWLEDGMENTS

Marin Sorescu, "This Hour," from *Born in Utopia: an Anthology of Modern and Contemporary Romanian Poetry*. Carmen Firan and Paul Doru Magur, with Edward Foster, eds. Talisman House, 2006.

William James, *The Principles of Psychology*, 1890; Dover edition 1950.

Camera Obscura, photographs by Abelardo Morell, introduction by Luc Sante, Bullfinch Press, 2004.

Leggi nel verde alloro, Vivaldi's *Orlando Furioso*, Act 2, Scene 14: "Read on the green laurel tree" carved into the living bark.

"Heterotopias are..." https: // schloss-post dot com/heterotopia

Li Shurui, "Seeing Mountains, Seeing Water," *Experimental Beijing: Gender and Globalization in Chinese Contemporary Art*, Sasha Su-Ling Welland. Duke University Press, 2018.

Wang Wei, "Deer Park," c. 750 AD.

"Fall" for Bill Viola ("He Weeps for You")

Psalm 94, 19: *In the multitude of my thoughts within me thy comforts delight my soul.*

Bernhard Siegert, *Cultural Techniques: Grids, Filters, Doors, and Other Articulations of the Real*, translated by Geoffrey Winthrop Young. Fordham University Press, 2015.

Cornelius Cardew, editor. *Scratch Music*. The MIT Press, 1974.

Thomas Nail, *Lucretius I: An Ontology of Motion*. Edinburgh University Press, 2018.

"Because of the light, because of the snow. The snow is a form of light. I wrote my last book of poetry, *Beginning and End of Snow*, with the memories and images of autumns and winters in New England." *The Paris Review* interview by Sasha Guppy, Summer 1994.

Thomas Aquinas, *Summa Theologica*. New York, Benziger, 1947.

"Nonmetallic inorganic compounds" was the definition of "ceramics" given to me by my Uncle Bill, aeronautical engineer working at the time on materials for supersonic aircraft.

Nathan Isgur was a fellow student in the 1963 National Science Foundation Summer Program in mathematics at the University of Texas.

Friedrich Nietzsche, *The Gay Science*, translated by Walter Kaufmann. Vintage Books, 1974.

The many people I should acknowledge for influences upon these poems include Sister M. Genevieve, O.P., John MacNamara, Stanley Plumly, Wayne Dodd, David Johnson, Carolyn Kizer, Donald Revell, Anna Rabinowitz, Jan Aronson, Meifu Wang, Mia Mulvey, and Beth Nugent and in both specific and general ways, always, Linda and Nic.

*

"Midmourning" appeared in *Mississippi Review*, Fall 2021.

"Body Parts" appeared in *Conjunctions 69*.

"Partial" and "A Change in Climate" appeared in *Jubilat* #35.

"Three Meditations on Matter" and "Where to Live" appeared in *Seneca Review*, Spring 2019.

"Phrase Book," "Applied Astronomy," and "Argument and Value, X and Y" appeared in issue 10 of *Clade Song*.

"Danses Sacrée et Profane (Debussy 1904)," "Secret Sins of the Light," and "They are Like Grass" appeared in *Peripheries*, Spring 2020.

"Thingness. A Many Body Problem" and "Phrase Book" appeared in *Visible Binary*. Fall 2021.

Bin Ramke's first book was a Yale Younger Poets selection. Since then he has published a dozen more, as well as having edited over eighty books for a university press. He was editor of the *Denver Quarterly* for some twenty years and has taught at Columbus State University in Georgia, the University of Denver, and on occasion since 1999 at the School of the Art Institute of Chicago. He continues to write, teach, and live in Denver with Linda and Nic.

Earth on Earth
Bin Ramke

Cover art by Mia Mulvey

Cover and interior typeface TT Marxiana

Cover and interior design by adam b. bohannon

Printed in the United States
by Books International, Dulles, Virginia
On Glatfelter 50# Cream Natures Book 440 ppi
Acid Free Archival Quality Recycled Paper

Publication of this book was made possible in part by gifts from
Katherine & John Gravendyk in honor of Hillary Gravendyk,
Francesca Bell, Mary Mackey, and The New Place Fund

Omnidawn Publishing
Oakland, California
Staff and Volunteers, Fall 2021

Rusty Morrison & Ken Keegan, senior editors & co-publishers
Kayla Ellenbecker, production editor & poetry editor
Rob Hendricks, editor for *Omniverse*, marketing, fiction & post-pub publicity
Sharon Zetter, poetry editor & book designer
Liza Flum, poetry editor
Matthew Bowie, poetry editor
Anthony Cody, poetry editor
Jason Bayani, poetry editor
Gail Aronson, fiction editor
Laura Joakimson, marketing assistant for Instagram & Facebook, fiction editor
Ariana Nevarez, marketing assistant & *Omniveres* writer, fiction editor
Jennifer Metsker, marketing assistant